Kham '

C000090108

Kham Tribes of Rolpa

Hit Bahadur Thapa

PILGRIMS PUBLISHING
◆ Varanasi ◆

Kham Tribes of Rolpa
Hit Bahadur Thapa

Published by:
PILGRIMS PUBLISHING

An imprint of:
PILGRIMS BOOK HOUSE
(Distributors in India)
B 27/98 A-8, Nawabganj Road
Durga Kund, Varanasi-221010, India
Tel: 91-542- 2314060
Fax: 91-542-2312456
E-mail: pilgrims@satyam.net.in
Website: www.pilgrimsbooks.com

Edited by Christohper N Burchett
Layout by Roohi Burchett

ISBN: 81-7769-582-7

Printed in India at Pilgrim Press Pvt. Ltd. Lalpur Varanasi

Contents

Introduction

Nepal is a resplendent country with its enchanting snow clad mountains and diversified cultures well known for harmonious co-existence of multiethnic and indigenous communities.

After 1990, a new awakening surged up among all tribes, ethnic and indigenous communities in the country.

The new constitution framed in 1990 gave a new social environment for these marginalized and suppressed communities to assert their social, cultural, linguistic and to some extent political rights under the nose of the changing governments at the center.

Most of these communities have mobilized themselves on the basis of their common language and cultural habits.

The Kham tribe of Rolpa also could not remain untouched by the changing world under the world wide social movement for tribal or community identity.

Through the meager efforts by writing this book on the Tribe of Rolpa, I think I have done my job in asserting the new tribal identity for the Kham community. It serves to identify the Kham community as a new community emerging in the country and we need to pay a little heed to this.

I will feel honored if my little efforts of writing this book will pave the way for the opening of new doors of identity for my community and work as an indispensable guide for those researchers willing to delve into the insight on the Kham community and their culture.

I am thankful to Pilgrims Book House that readily accepted my manuscript for publication. I also extend my gratitude to my friend Durlav and all those who inspired me to write this book.

Oral history on origin of the Kham Tribes

According to an old legend, which has been handed down from generations to generations till date, a Kham woman had become pregnant in a certain Kham village near Ugahm Maoikot in Rukum district long ago. When the woman's parents came to know about her pregnancy, they asked her how she became pregnant. The woman at first did not disclose her clandestine relation with a stranger who had impregnated her. But when her parents including the villagers insisted upon her to disclose the name of the stranger, she decided to tell them about the stranger at last. She told them that she would often meet a strange type of man in the darkness of night. He would go away early next morning leaving her in her slumber without telling her where he had come from and where was he going.

His coming in the night and sleeping with her was merely a coincidence now and then. But since she had already met him at least three or four times in similar situations, she could not resist his approach. He had impregnated her in the course of time. As a result, she was worried whether he would come back again to accept her as his wife or not.

After knowing this the villagers and the woman's parents told her a plan to find out who her husband was. According to the new plan made by the villagers, one day during the night when the same stranger happened to come to meet his lover, she received him without giving him any doubts of the plan and before he left the next morning, she tied a string of thread to one of his legs.

The next morning as the man rose and took to his heels, the woman unloosened the limitless strings of thread behind him. As the man walked across the fields and forest the string kept on stretching from the hands of the woman in the cowshed.

The long string of thread stopped when the man too reached his dwelling place. But by this time the man was out of sight of the villagers and the woman. As the string of thread stopped moving any more, she called her parents and the villagers. She told them what had happened the previous night indicating the long trail of the string on the ground.

The villagers then followed the trails of the string whereever it went. The string had passed through the maze of bushes, trees, and deep forest and through the water and mud till it reached the mid portion of high rocky precipice that lay in front of them right across the river.

Then the amazed villagers and parents of the impregnated woman shouted across the river, "Who are you? Come forward. Why did you impregnate our daughter?"

At this a strange voice came from inside the cave in the rocky precipices, " You don't worry about my child and wife, I have managed to send some domestic food materials and animals with which my wife and child would be able to fend for them selves in the future. My men will be arriving there before you within a few seconds." said the strange voice from inside the deep dark cave across the rock.

No sooner had he finished saying his words than there arrived several tiny men carrying loads of domestic materials and animals.

Those animals included cows, goats and chickens whilst the domestic materials included ploughs and a few baskets full of grain and seeds.

The stranger neither appeared nor spoke any further words.

After this the villagers returned to their homes along with the pregnant woman and gave her the permission to give birth to her baby. Since then the new generation of descendants were known as *Sutpahare Rokas* and *Ghirties*.

Arrival of a hunter from the North

There is a folk tale about the arrival of a hunter from the north. According to the folk tale, long ago, a strange hunter strolled into the region (which the Kham tribes inhabit today) from the northern side. Whether he came from central Asia or not is unknown. However, his arrival from the north could indicate towards a certain degree of proximity in the civilization of Kham people with that of the Mongol civilization and development in Central Asia.

The hunter had an arrow and bow in his hands. Arrows and bows are one of the hallmarks of Kham tribal culture today, which testifies to a certain degree that the strange hunter could have been one of the earliest ancestors of the Kham tribes.

One day, while the hunter was roaming about in the forest, he killed a bird with his arrow, roasted it on the fire and sat down to eat it. However, while he was operating on the bird's chest and intestine, he found a few grains in the intestine. He could not recognize what they were. So, he just buried those grains in the ground to see what happened to them later on. He then returned to his shelter. After some days, when he returned to the same place, to his great surprise, he found that the grain he had buried into the ground had sprouted into eatable crops. This incident taught the hunter how to grow crops. He then settled down in the same place and to follow an started agricultural life. In the course of time his descendants came to be known as *Jhethi Paryal Rokas* in this region.

The folk legends of two Shaman brothers

According to another legend heard in the villages, one of the sources of the origin of Kham tribes dates back to those primordial days when two shaman brothers lived together. Of the two brothers, the younger one was more cunning and mischievous. Both of these brothers had sons too. The elder brother had five sons, who used to fight with the sons of the younger brother. The sons of the younger brother were endowed with more invisible powers of shamanism, while the five sons of the elder brother were less expert in wielding the power of shamanism. Taking undue advantage of this situation, the sons of the younger brother often used to torment the five elder brothers by pricking them with needles using the power of shamanism. In this risky game of spells, the three sons of the elder brother were killed by the sons of the younger brother, which really alarmed the the two remaining brothers.

One day, while the elder brother was on his deathbed, his two desperate sons approached him in a gloomy mood and lamented over the bleak future they could foresee after his death. They were dismayed that they might also have to meet with the same fatal end of their lives as their three innocent brothers met with at the evil hands of their younger brothers.

At this, the dying old man sympathized with them and soothed their hearts by saying that if they would do a task as he told them they would secure their future from their evil brothers.

The old man said, "Do as I tell you. First of all, as soon as I die, take me to the place in the forest where your evil brothers have kept the sharp snare ready for the animals to be entrapped. Put my dead body across the snare and make it appear as if my body was trapped into their snare as I was strolling in the forest. The next day, go to your cousins and report the matter to them that I have not returned from the forest last night.

Bring them to me where I lay dead in the forest in search of me. Once they find me on their snare and dead due to their snare, they would be ashamed of themselves. Their father would ask you to demand anything in return for my death. At this you can ask them to give you the open lands in compensation for my death. This way you can part from your evil brothers and lead your lives in peace in the open lands. The old man then died saying these words to his two sons. The two sons immediately did the same as their father had told them. When the evil brothers saw the dead body of elder uncle they were shocked. At last they agreed to give away the open lands except those covered by the forest. They also made a compromise to separate from each other forever and never to meet again.

On the day of distribution of land, the evil brothers parted from the two elder brothers by using the fence of *Chitra*. Initially, they erected one chitra, then another, till seven chitras were erected behind which the evil brothers hid themselves, never again to meet their elder brothers in the future.

The legend says since then they have never met with each other. These two elder brothers who started living on the open lands became the forefathers of Kham people, while the evil brothers became the ancestors of invisible shamans living in the jungle.

The Kham people also opine that the ancient Khams learnt the art of shamanism from their younger brothers of jungle. Some of the villagers opine that these lost brothers of the Kham tribes are occasionally seen as jungle man, jungle shaman or yeti. These creatures are usually found bare footed, unclad with just hairy bodies, of short stature. Their language is difficult to understand. It is said that the jungle shamans survive on earthworms.

Once a villager who disappeared for more than five or six months was found sleeping across the rock just suspended in the air without a base to hold on. With great difficulty the man was brought down and brought home. When he regained his

18

consciousness back he narrated how a tiny and frail man suddenly took him somewhere and kept him for those days, who also taught him to heal the various types of disease in a natural way while was kept in a rocky cave. This man ultimately became a natural born shaman who could heal the diseases in the village.

When asked about where he had gone to and for how long and what was he fed on till then? He said that a little man took him to strange place inside a cave and fed him with the soup of earthworm. While eating the food, he was asked to use the opposite side of the palm (palms upside down). The villagers believe that that little man is the descendent of the same brothers who had parted from their elder brothers long ago and opted to live in the dark and forest area according to the pre-condition set at the time of separation from their brothers.

According to the condition if the two brothers saw one another at any place, only one should see the other. That is to say, at the meeting point, if the elder brother would see younger brother at first then the younger brother should not be able to see the elder brother.

If the younger brother could see the elder, then the elder brother would not be able to see the younger brother. The kham people still believe in the legends today.

The Khams living near the dense forest have sometime heard the sound of a drum played by shamans in the forest.

It is said one of the villagers one day had seen a tiny man looking almost like a shaman dressed in his uniform and sitting all alone on a huge stone near by a spring in the dense forest. The villager was frightened to see the tiny man so he went back home and returned to the same place with his friends. But the tiny shaman had disappeared.

It is also believed that if anyone happens to see the tiny man, he should have enough courage to snatch away anything that the little man might possess at that time. Otherwise he would be sick and might die as well. But to snatch away anything from the tiny man is not so easy. One must struggle with the tiny man.

The legend says one day, a certain man suddenly saw a tiny man walking in front of him with a rope in his hands. The man reached behind the tiny man and tried to snatch away the rope from the tiny man. Then there ensued a battle between the two. They started grappling with each other. At last the man overpowered the tiny man and took possession of the rope and made his way home. The man then walked away without looking back at the tiny man.

There is a belief that if the man had looked back at the tiny man, he might have died on reaching home. But the man already knew this, so he did not look back at all. After reaching home the man kept the rope in a room. Later be became a rich man in the village.

Significance of 'Kham'

The word kham means "power" as it represents the pedigree of the ancient Tartars of Mongol origin who dispersed in different directions of Asia and world in search of new conquered kingdoms and wealth.

The Kham tribes are perhaps the descendants of Mongol Tartars who were warriors by nature and blood. One of the branches of the Tartar Mongols had subjugated Hungary a European country. A Magyar team that had visited Nepal in 1999 had acknowledged that the Tartar Mongols had subjugated their ancestors. The Magyar team members during their visit to Rolpa also acknowledged that the old swords found in most of the houses of the Kham people are the swords wielded by the Tartar Mongols against Magyars in the historical fight in Hungary. This clearly indicates that there is no room left for anyone that khams are the descendants of Mongol Tartars.

One of the legends relates that Khams might have come from Tibet during the early period of Mongol civilization. To verify this fact, even today Tibet has a provincial territory known 'Kham Province' which also indicates the early history of the Khams having descended from the Tartars, the most fiery warriors that the world has ever known.

History

The Kham tribes were independent tribes leading their own tribal lives in the Himalayan region. Their kingdom extended from the present Mahakali region in the west to the Rapti zone in the east in the past. However there are no chronicled evidences to prove it. The medieval history of the Karnali region testifies that the Kham people had cordial relations with the kingdoms of Kashmir in the past.

The ancestors of the Kham people had to face frequent attacks of Khas kings and chieftains from across the border in the Mahakali region to the west. The ancestors of the Kham people are believed to have fought with their Khas enemies in the Mahakali region several times. The Khas kings were defeated many times but the wars continued for several decades.

One of the wars between the Kham and Khas people is believed to have lasted for nearly 42 years during which hundreds of Khas and Kham soldiers were decimated.

At the end of the 42-year-old war, the Kham kings were defeated and the Khas kings subjugated the small kingdoms of Kham mercilessly in the Karnali and Mahakali region. After the defeat the of Kham kings, Khas soldiers swept and crushed the areas of Kham people. Hundreds of Kham people escaped to the eastern parts of Nepal. Many of them settled in the areas like Rolpa and Rukum and its vicinity to escape the wrath of Khas soldiers.

That's why we find only the negligible population of Kham people in the Karnali and Mahakali region nowadays.

Later the Khas kings and Kham kings agreed to an understanding to live in peace and harmony after the Kham kings agreed pay some retribution to the Khas kingdom at Jumla annually. Since then the Khas kingdom was confined to Jumla region from where the Khas rulers started ruling over the Kham people and other tribes in the region.

As long as the Khas ruled from Jumla the Kham people lived under them. Later again another phase of the unification campaign was started by Prithvi Narayan Shah from the Gorkha kingdom that also started a series of traumatic experiences for the Kham people.

This time the Kham people were assimilated into the present Nepal by subjugating their homelands during the perilous period of so called unification in Nepal.

The present history testifies to one of the historical incidences wherein one of the Kham kings popularly known as Bokshe Jhand in the Rukum region was killed by Khas enemies after making him tumble into a big pit and killing him by pelting stones at him in a conspiracy hatched against him long before the process of unification started in the region.

The small kingdoms of kham people had fiercely defied the forcible unification of kham kingdoms into the present Nepal. In whatever way the modern historians depict the historical scenario of the time of unification period. However, if any of the kham tribal chiefs are to be asked about the ordeal of that period, they would describe it as the most painful for the kham people. In fact the process of assimilation forced the kham people to forget their language, culture and history and loose a greater portion of land that they had occupied in the history before the Khas subjugated them and the unification process. The chief shamans of this region were slain for defying new orders of administration. All other shamans were forbidden to use their local kham language in their cultural rites and ceremonies. They were forced to use the Nepali language. The kham people were also forbidden to sing songs in their own languages. Ultimately most of the kham tribes started adopting the khas language as the language of public contact. So even today, these people sing songs in Nepali despite having their own rich language to sing the songs. However, the kham people should take pride in the fact that the local places, villages towns are still known by the kham language such as Libang, Thabang, Pobang, Ghusbang etc. The names of the these places are more than thousand years old which indicate towards early history and civilization of kham tribes that flourished in this region.

Population and Region

The kham population can be estimated to be in the range of 4,00,000 to 5,00,000 in the districts of Rolpa, Rukum and its adjacent districts including those residing in karnali region the far western part of Nepal.

Cutural Traditions

As soon as a child is born, the household members cook a handful of *Hamsya* in the name of the child who is born. This is because of the general belief that the child without *Hamsya* may feel hungry in his later life. Though the *Hamsya* is not fed to the child, it has become the tradition of kham people in this region.

The *Nauran* of the child is observed after three days and the child is given food three months onwards. The mother also starts doing domestic chores after three days. On the day of *Nauran* the villagers and relatives come to visit the child with rice, oil, cocks or hens. The kham shaman priest gives a new name to the child and sees the horoscope of the child.

A certain amount of rice is cooked, and then ghee is mixed into it. This food is distributed among the attendants of the *nauran* ceremony. Meanwhile, a big cock is also killed and cooked to mix its meat into the rice already mixed with the ghee. Then all the spices are mixed into it. When everything is ready, the mixed rice is put into a large plate and arranged in pyramid shape. And just on the top of the rice, the head of a cock is kept to make it appear as if it is standing erect. Then this plate of rice is placed on a *Nangli* in his hands a few inches above the ground across the door and the *Nangli* is scraped undernath its surface with the help of the fingers of the dead cock. Then every household member is made to cross the door three times to and fro. After this rite is completed the mixed rice is distributed among all the people gathered on the occasion. Then each person visits the child, sees his face and returns home by bestowing their blessings or gifts on the child. Some people also give money into the hands of the child. The whole day, the invited guests drink and eat then disperse to their respective houses.

The of Purvodai

There is a typical cultural tradition among the kham people. According to this tradition, the dancing group of *Singaro* comes to the house where the new child is born. The dancing groups visit each house and asks for the *Purvodai* during the *tihar* festival. If the baby is a son then the parents of the baby have to give certain amount of money along with other eatables to the dancing groups. If the baby is a daughter then the group is pacified with whatever amount of money or eatables provided by the parents. The dancing group blesses the child with long life and prosperity before leaving the house on getting the demanded money and eatables.

Marriage Tradition

Among the kham tribes the custom of dragging away the girl of ones choice is one the most popular customs. However, nowadays this practice is disappearing from the society as the Maoists have discarded this practice.

All the same this practice reminds us of the practices of our ancestors, who used to drag away the girl of their choice to marry.

Most of the boys and girls elope after falling in love. Besides this, the arranged marriage is also in practice. According to the kham tradition, the kham youth must marry his maternal uncle's daughter. However, nowadays the society has started changing its outlook. It is not compulsory. The society is far more liberal and open in the sense that a divorced man or woman has the freedom to remarry. The man and woman are free to choose their life partners.

Before going to ask for the hand of the girl, the boy's parents and few elderly people gather and discuss the approach to be made. A cock is killed for *Basin batra*. This is predicted by seeing the heart of the dead cock. The elderly people know how to read the different signs that appear on the heart and intestine of the cock. Sometimes the *Basin batra* clearly indicates that their approach to the girl would be responded in a positive manner. And the same *Basin Batra* can indicate the total negative approach too.

After seeing the *Basin batra* the elderly group go to the girl's house. They talk to the girl's parents and elderly people. They at last ask them to take the consent of the girl. Then the boy gives *Shahi Masha* to the girl. This is considered to be a proposal from the boy's side. Now the girl has the right to reject or accept the *Shahi Masha*. If she accepts it the engagement follows. The boy's side offers a large cock to be killed on the occasion. This custom is called *Kukara karai*.

Once again the heart of the dead cock is read to see the sign of good and bad. Then both the parents and boy's relatives eat and drink together to enjoy the occasion of engagement.

After *Kukra karai* the girl is allowed to stay at her parent's house until the date of marriage is fixed. This period may range from six months to one year. The marriage can be fixed in the following days too. Until the girl comes home, the boy's parents have to carry *jung* consisting of drinks and eatables to the girl's parents. In the meantime, if the girl elopes away with somebody else, then her parents pay the compensation of the *Shahimasha* by paying certain amount of money to the boy's parents.

The marriage day is fixed by the *Kham jaisi* on the marriage day. Some of the boy's relatives and the *jaisi* go and bring the girl from her parent's house. The *jaisi* fixes the exact moment and hour during which the bride should enter the bridegroom's house. So, before the arrival of the bride the main door of the bridegroom's house is decorated properly. Bronze jars filled with pure water are installed on both sides of the door. Inside the door, three or four spots of cow dung are kept on which the bride steps and bridegroom stamps his feet while entering the house. The moment the bride steps inside the door, a man shoots rifle into the open air outside. Inside the house the bride and bridegroom are made to sit together. In a moment the bride is asked to wear *khyo bhe* . Then both the pairs offer a piece of red and white strips of clothes called *Dhaja* to the *Dhuri khamba.*

After that both apply the *Tika* to each other's foreheads. Then the bridegroom's parents and relatives apply the same *tika* to the bride and bridegroom one by one. Then while eating, the pair must be together and both of them should add or leave nothing to the first food serving in their respective plates.

The next day, the *janti* moves towards the bride's ancestral house *Maita* with a long march of retinue. The *janti* carries with them various loads of foods and drinks known as *Pokas* for the girl's parents and relatives.

On the way to *Maita* the bride's head is covered with a white stripe of clothe called *Nanfa* while the long strip of white cloth covering her back side from shoulder to the shin is called *barki*. The bride groom's head is covered with dhoro while he has his waist wrapped up by *whampo* into which he keeps his *Kuthuminar*. The pair carries a small kettle filled with the jar and millet, which is thrown on the way from time to time and distributed to passersby and viewers. While moving, it is the *jaisi* who goes in front followed by the bride and bridegroom. *Damai* who are equiped with traditional musical instruments may also accompany the Janti.

In this way, the Janti reaches the Maita. On their arrival they are welcomed into the house. The bride and bridegroom along with the jaisi are made to sit together at a place. The Janti is fed with food and drinks. Usually at night, the Janti dances the whole night. The parents usually offer bronze made utensils in return for the Poka they received. After the *tika tauli* the janti is granated permission to depart. The janti is garlanded with flowers. The son-in-law of the bridegroom's side holds the *lo* and *Daiti* in his hands to dance with it on the way back home. The janti moves slowly with dancing mood and reaches home within the specified time. After that night the marriage rituals are is over. However, the janti along with the bride and bridegroom should return to the girl's Maita after few days.

They stay at Maita for one night and return home. Then almost all the marriage customs are considered to be over.

Death Rites

Among the kham tribes, when a person is dead, the elderly people look after him until the relatives of the deceased arrive. If the relatives from far off places have to come then the dead man can be looked after for two to three days and nights.

As soon as the person is dead Bato is stretched across the road near the dead man's house, which symbolizes that some one in the house is dead. Then Damai is called and asked to beat the drum called that indicates that some one is dead. The dead body is covered with a cloth. But before the dead body is carried away it is massaged with mustard oil. Then the dead body is made to wear his new clothes that he loved the most. After he is dressed up in his new clothes, he is wrapped up on to the poles of bamboo. The relatives continue to bring liquor and wood to support the household members of the dead man. They can also bring white strips of cloth to add to what is already stretched. While carrying the body towards the *khaddar*, the Damai plays tunes of sorrowful tone on his flute.

The other musical instruments such as *Jhayali* and *Bhonker* also follow along with the corpse up to the cremation ground. Usually, the dead man's sons, nephews and son-in-laws should lift the body.

Both men and women go to the cemetery ground. The Bato is lifted by the blacksmiths who take away the bato after the man is buried or cremated. In a few cases the dead body can be cremated. It is customary that women who are closely related to the dead should weep in a rhyming tune like a song while the body is being carried away to the cremation ground. The weeping women usually follow after the corpse of the dead man.

The relative women weeping in a rhyming tone with sorrowful and tearful eyes narrate the whole story of how they were related to the dead man during his life. The weeping women lament over the loss of their loved one who is leaving them in this world.

Along with the corpse the dead man's most loving possessions like the pots or any belongings of the house are also carried to the cremation ground.

If the dead is a shaman usually his books or tools he used are carried along with his body. If the man is a scholar then his books are carried with him.

After reaching the burial ground, the dead man is prepared to be buried. So, the ground dug out. When the ground is ready, the body is put over it. Fire is put across the mouth of the dead. Then all along with his dearest belongings the man is buried. Usually a few slabs of stones are put across the ground and especially one large stone is erected over the head side of the body.

While returning home, the people must purify themselves by breaking an egg at the cross road. The household members of the dead do not eat salt for at least three days. The sons usually shave their heads to mourn the death of their father while the daughters bind up or keep open their hairs in a different style.

After three days the purifying ceremony begins in the house of the dead. On the occasion, a buffalo, sheep or a pig is killed. A handful of the meat is also distributed to every person attending the ceremony. This ceremony usually breaks off on the bank of a river.

The home is cleaned with cow's dung and every one enjoys the drinks and food. On the same evening, a shaman is invited to do the performance according to which the dead man's spirit is pacified. From the next day, the house is completely purified.

Installing wooden carved pillars in the memory of the dead

The kham tribes have been able to retain this age-
old tradition of installing wooden carved pillars in
memory of the dead. The dead person's physical
features are carved into a wooden pillar and
installed on the side of the main road near by the
people's resting platforms. When wooden pillars
are not installed, large and long pieces of stones
are embedded into the ground in the name of the
dead, usually at the public resting places on the
main roads. These are built in the memory of the
dead ones. And just on the opposite side to the
edge of the road, the wooden carved pillars are
installed to commemorate the dead persons. Their
Maitees or parental household members also
commemorate the daughters who were married

and died long ago by installing a few slabs of stones, so that the spirit of the dead daughters may quench their thirst while visiting their parents.

These wooden pillars last for more than a century. Hence some of these pillars are as old as a hundred years.

Customary ways and habits

Receiving a guest with a warm heart is the tradition of the kham tribes. The guest must be offered homemade fermented liquor called *Jhanr* on arrival of the guest. If the house does not have jhanr then any other liquor is provided to the guest as a sign of respect and honor. Traditionally making the guest drunk is considered to be the matter of satisfaction on the part of the host. If the guest is an important person and has come for the first time, then a cock or hen is killed in his honor. When serving the food and drinks to the guest, it is customary to serve at least two times or more or else the host feels offended. So the guest even if not hungry has to accept the second serving of food or drinks, at least a small quantity.

On the other hand, the guest also has to pretend that he does not want to eat more. But the host insists that the guest takes more of the servings. The guests are made to sit on a Lo. If the guest is VIP then the blanket made of sheep's wool is spread over the Lo for the guests. Before serving the food the guests are made to wash their hands in a large bowl. The hosts usually eat after the guests have eaten.

Woman as the head of the family

Among the kham tribes the women are still considered to be the head of the family to decide on important matters of the family. The women carry equal loads with men and work harder than the men in the fields. The women are free to move anywhere. They are not treated as subordinate to men in the kham community.

Main Foods

Kham tribes mainly depend on maize, wheat, potato, and millet as the foodstuffs. Rice is grown in a limited quantity. So rice is eaten only on the occasion of great festivals. However nowadays gradually the villagers are getting the excess to the markets nearby and are able to buy the rice and eat it as and when they like.

Besides this, several other natural vegetables like mushrooms and wild plants are eaten by kham people. Kham people eat chicken, mutton, buffalo, beef and pork. But pork and beef are not allowed inside the house as it is considered to be impure in kham customs. So any one eating pork or beef should enter the house after purifying his body by applying a plant called *pati* on his body. Otherwise it is believed that the ancestors would get angry and make the household members sick if the house is contaminated with pork or beef.

Domestic Utensils used

Kham people generally take pride in having utensils made up of bronze. Only a few years back these people did not know about steel and glass. Now some of them use these factory made utensils too. The people still use the wooden bottles called 'Theka' to collect the milk, curd, ghee and water. Besides this the Bronje and silver plates and bowls are considered to be the domestic utensils of homely pride. The larger bowls made of bronze are used to make liquor, food and collect water respectively.

The wooden plate pai is also used to eat from.

Various other utensils use by the kham people are kodalo, Rangil, khukuri, mandal, etc.

Types of Houses

The Kham tribes of Rolpa and Rukum have become used to living in the terrai areas of the hilly region. They usually make small thatched houses. However, the families with of good source income also make two storied houses roofed by slab of stone cut into shape by the mason. Traditionally built houses have arch shaped main pillars at the entrance of the house. Even thatched houses have two stories. People live on the ground floor while grains are stored on the second storey. The ground floor of the house is generally divided into three of four parts. The first part is the entrance. The entrance is also found spacious enough to seat a few household members. The second part is the largest room that spares two parts in it and leaves space for a fireplace right in the middle of the room. The space near by the entrance is meant for guests, while the other is for household member to sleep on.

Religious Traditions

The central point of religious faith among the kham
of Rolpa and Rukum is that of animistic and bon
tradition in worshiping their deities like 12 Brahas
and 22 Bajus.

12 Brahas are worshipped at *Brahathan* and
22 Bajus are worshipped at *Bajuthan*. Along with
this the other deity worshipped include the *Siddha*
who is worshipped at *Siddhathan*.

And the ancestors of the kham are known and
worshiped at *pitrathan*, usually made of three
stones with its wide-open mouth at the front side
where the ancestors are offered new grain during
harvest.

Usually a Dhami does all sorts of worshiping
in these thans. A kham woman can also do the
work of worshiping at these thans provided she
has turned into a '*Dhamaeni*'.

The Dhamies and Dhamenise usually sport long hair. At the time of worship the Dhamies and Dhamenies and dressed in white robes and dance around the thans with bells in their hands. As they move around the thans their bodies shiver terribly.

A Dhami usually draws the various lines with maize flour before the than. Generally on every occasion of worshiping of Braha, Sidha or Bajues a sheep is sacrificed at the altar of the than. Thans are usually found adjacent to a pond. No one is allowed to take a bath in this pond.

In this connection, the Brahathan and the pond situated in ward no 7 of tribhuwan Nagar Palika, near Ghorahi town in Dang district is considered to be the chief Barathan and the Pond. The pond is also known by the name of Barahakune Daha.

According the chief priest of this than, Jasram Gharty, the 12 Brahas and 22 Bajus deities had emerged from this pond and dispersed to different directions towards the west and east of Nepal.

Folk legends on the origin of the 12 Brahasand and the 22 Baju deities

According to Jasram Gharty of Barahkune Daha, 12 Brahas and 22 Bajus had emerged from this pond. The eldest braha went to stay in Jaljala in Rukum district while the youngest braha remained in Dang district, while other brothers and sisters dispersed in different directions to take hold of each than at various places which are yet to be found out. But most of the thans they occupy can be found mainly within Rapti zone.

The Gharty families living around the Barahkune daha know much about the legends of origin of Barahakune Daha and Brahathan. According to them long ago, there was no pond. It was a valley like place with dense forest. It was a grazing ground for sheep brought down from Piunthan district. When the sheep would come down to graze there, the sheep herds used to make shelters and stay there for few months. Once there were twelve sheep sheds. One night an old man with white hair appeared in the dreams of an old shepherd sleeping under the sheep shed and said, " all of you go to the other place tomorrow because tomorrow night a heavy rainfall will occur and this place will be turned into a pond." The next day, the old shepherd narrated the whole story to his colleagues. But they did not believe in his story that appeared to be a fairy tale. But he went to the top of the hillock nearby and stayed there during the night, while his friends spent the night in the same valley. That very night exactly as predicted by the hairy old man, the whole valley was turned into a pond full of water due to a heavy rainfall. The shepherds along with their sheep were drowned in the pond, which was created by the heavy overnight rainfall. Only the old shepherd that had acted according to the predictions had survived in the incident.

Now once the water pond was created, the people still did not know much about its importance. Whenever anyone would come near the pond, the voice of cocks and sheep would be heard in the pond. Sometime the people would go there to swim and bathe.

One day, the daughter of a gharty family had gone there to take a bath in the pond. As she was bathing in the pond, she was drowned and disappeared into the pond for many days. The girl's parents and the villagers came to know about what had happened to the girl in the pond. They were worried but couldn't do anything to save her from the pond. One day, suddenly the girl appeared from the pond and went to her parent's house to meet them. Her parents were surprised and overjoyed to find her again in front of them.

The girl's parents asked her how she had disappeared in the pond and how she had survived for so many days? She replied that she was married to Braha in the pond. They asked where her husband was? Then she replied that her husband was on the way to their house. Then within a fraction of seconds, a swarm of bees came on the site of discussion and took her away from the house of her parents.

After this incident, the girl's mother became anxious to see her three grand children in the pond. So she went to the pond and shouted the name of her daughter. At this her daughter came out of the pond and asked her mother why she had come there? The mother asked her how many children she had given birth to? At this the daughter said that she was the mother of three children. Then her mother wished to see her grand children. At this her daughter told her that once they came in front of her she would be scared at their sight. But her mother insisted her daughter to show her her grand children at any cost.

At this the girl dived into the pond and brought with her one of her children and showed it to her mother near the pond.

But as soon as her mother got hold of the grand child, she screamed in terror and dropped the child on the ground because the child was in the form of a serpent. It is said that while the child was dropped the child had broken one of its legs.

Then the girl picked up her child and dived into the pond never to come back again to meet her parents. Since then the girl has not been found anywhere in the surrounding area.

Many years after this incident the water of the pond started decreasing slowly and there appeared a large tree that had the appearance of a snake. A few cooking pots were also available below the tree. The travelers passing the in nights under the tree would cook the is food in the same pots and then continue their journey. The travelers would not steal the pots from there that place.

But one day, a greedy traveler stole the cooking utensils and tried to escape from there. But he could not get out of that area. He would walk a few steps ahead but return to the same tree again and again. At last, the greedy man left those utensils and went ahead. This time he was able to return to his house. Since then, those utensils disappeared from the place and never appeared again.

Ever since the appearance of the tree, the brahthan was established at the root of the tree.

A few bells were hung from the branches of the tree.

Much later a village chief or Mukhya thought of felling the tree and building a temple instead of the Brahthan. So, he asked some people to cut the tree one day. The Mukhya was warned in a dream not to cut the tree. But he got the tree cut by the people. It is said that the man who gave the first stroke of axe to the tree had vomited blood next day and died instantly. And the Mukhya who had ordered for the tree to be cut down also died after a few days as his house caught fire. And the rest of the people who had assisted in cutting the tree had suffered from a dreadful disease. So the villagers fearing the wrath of the Braha diety built the Brahthan in the same place again.

Since this pond had emerged on the last day of the month of Poush, even today the people celebrate a big fair on the last day of Poush as Barahkune fair.

Glossary

Sutpahare Rokas and *Ghirties;* Here Sut means a 'thread' while pahare means 'rocky'. The word Sutpahare Rokas and Ghirties refers to the clan of kham Rokas and Ghirties whose origin is linked with the thread of the rock or whose pedigree dates back to the cave.

Jhethi Paryal Rokas; Here Jhethi means the eldest and paryal means the family. Hence jhethi Paryal Rokas means the eldest family clans among the Kham Rokas.

Chitra; a waterproof roof made out of local bamboo.

Usual cowsheds are made out of chitra in the village.

Hamsya; a handful of rice or wheat cooked just before the child is born. It is believed that Hamsya would make the child not feel too much hungry in his youth.

Nauran- birth day of a child

Nangli- a bamboo woven domestic handy utensil used to separate the grains of crops.

Purvodai- a tradition of demanding money on the occasion of a child born in a kham family.

Singaro- Male dancers masked as girls to dance on the occasion of festival Tihar one of the festivals of Nepal. The dance is also known as 'Sorathi' in other parts of Nepal.

Tihar- Festival of lights celebrated in Nepal.

Basin batra, which means trying to find out the good or evil effect of the moment.

Shahi Masa -certain amount of money, usually in coins given to the girl to fix the marriage.

Kukara karai- means the girls has accepted the Shahi Masa and is ready to marry the boy.Both the sides happily celebrate the occasion by drinking and eating.

Jung -carrying drinks and eatables to the girl's house.

Kham jaisi-a kham priets appointed to perform the marriage rites.

khyo bhe-Means bridal dress worn by the bride.

Dhaja- red or black strip of clothes used to appease the kham family deity.

Dhuri khamba-main central pillar of the house

Tika- means applying a mixer of rice grains mixed in curd on the forehead.

Janti -crowd of people moving along with bride and bridegroom.

Maita-means the house of girl where she was born.

Pokas-means the foods and drinks demanded by the parents of the bride.

Nainfa- a head scarf use by the bride to cover her head on the occasion of marriage.

barki- a long white stripe of clothe used by the bride at the time of marriage to cover her head to shin area of the body.

Dhoro- a white strip of clothe wrapped around the head of the groom on the occasion of marriage.

whampo- a woolen stripe of clothes worn by the groom.

Kuthuminar - a khukuri sheath studded with silver and silver.

Damai- a man from khas community who plays music on flute on the occasion of marriage.

tika tauli- applying the mixer of rice grain and curd on the foreheads of bride and groom.

lo- a bamboo woven mattress used by the guests to sit on which is lifted and used to revolve at the tips of the fingers while dancing.

Daiti- a domestic utensils kept by the fire side on which the pots are placed for resting. This is used to dance with during a marriage ceremony.

Bato - a long strip of white clothe spread on the way towards the cremation ground in the name of the dead.

khaddar- a cremation ground

Jhayali- a handy musical instrument played by two hands

Bhonker- a long musical instrument played by blowing air into it.

Jhanr- homemade fermented liquor

pati- a plant used for purity and incense in religious ceremony.

Pai- a wooden plate to eat from

12 Brahas and 22 Bajus- the 12 brother deities and 22 sister deities of khams people whom they worshipp

Brahathan - a place to worship one of the 12 Braha deities.

Bajuthan- a place to worship one of the 22 sister deities of Khams.

Siddha- another kham deity

pitrathan- a place to worship the ancestors

Dhami- kham priests male

Dhamaeni - female priest

Barahakune Daha- a pond with 12 corners

About the author

Hit Bahadur Thapa was born in a small village of Uwa in Uwa Village Development Committee of Rolpa district in the year 1964 on the first of a December.

He shifted to India at an early age along with his father who was then employed in the Border Security Force.

He did his secondary and higher secondary education from India. He finished his BA in Elective English from the University of North Bengal in India in 1987.

He worked as a sailor in the Indian Navy for nearly three years. He then worked as an English teacher, principal in some schools. He was also actively engaged in the social mobilization of indigenous groups for the last one-decade. He now works as a journalist.